ENTERING THE DHARMA-DOOR

Of

BUDDHA

MINDFULNESS

ALSO BY THE VENERABLE XIAO PINGSHI

ENTERING THE DHARMA-DOOR

Of

BUDDHA
MINDFULNESS

XIAO PINGSHI

Wholesome Vision™

Entering the Dharma-Door of Buddha-Mindfulness

Copyright © 2016 by Wholesome Vision™

Published by Wholesome Vision™

1405 Bodega Way #5

Diamond Bar

CA 91765, USA

Tel: 1-909-638-7179

Fax: 1-626-839-5333

Website of Wholesome Vision:

www.wholesomevision.com

www.enlighten.org.tw

ISBN: 978-0-9972254-2-6

First U.S. Edition

About the Author

Born in 1944, the Venerable Master Xiao Pingshi (蕭平實) was raised in a farming family in central Taiwan. Seeking answers to the truth of human existence, he became a committed Buddhist disciple and practitioner in his forties, and in 1990 attained awakening to the True Mind via Chan contemplation and the aid of an incredible Dharma-door called "signless Buddha-mindfulness."

In 1997, Master Xiao established the Buddhist True Enlightenment Practitioners Association in order to offer different levels of Dharma classes to practitioners. Presently, the Association's practice centers have reached all major cities of Taiwan, and beyond to Hong Kong and the United States. Since the founding of the Association, Master Xiao has been giving weekly lectures on important Buddhist scriptures, such as the *Laṅkāvatāra Sūtra*, the *Śūraṅgama Sūtra*, the *Sūtra on Upāsaka Precepts*, the *Śrīmālādevī Siṃhanāda Sūtra*, the *Diamond Sūtra,* the *Lotus Sūtra*, and so forth.

To elucidate the Buddha Dharma and its stages of cultivation for all interested learners, Master Xiao has also published more than a hundred books on a wide range of Buddhist subjects. These include the combined cultivation of Chan and Pure Land, the realization of the Path to Liberation expounded in the *Āgamas*, the analysis of the profound Middle-Way teachings and the exegesis of key Consciousness-Only scriptures. All of his books emphasize the points that Buddhism is a path of personal realization and that realization can only come through a continual process of listening to, contemplating, and actual practice of the Buddha Dharma.

CONTENTS

ENTERING THE DHARMA-DOOR

Of

BUDDHA
MINDFULNESS

Reining In the Six Sense Faculties and Abiding in One Continuous Pure Thought

Buddha-mindfulness is a Dharma-door (Buddhist practice method) that accommodates practitioners of all capacities and fits especially well with today's busy and stressful lifestyle. It is easy to learn and can be taken up by people of all ages and backgrounds, from eighty-year-olds to three-year-olds, from college professors to street peddlers, and even those with little formal education.

With enough faith, everyone can respond to and derive benefits from this method according to his or her capacities. Practitioners who apply themselves diligently to the study of the Buddha Dharma, and carefully reflect upon the teachings, may even realize the True Mind and see the Buddha-nature by way of Buddha-mindfulness. Regrettably, a small number of people who regard themselves as having sharp faculties do not deign to practice Buddha-mindfulness. Consequently, they miss out on the wonderful benefits it can bring to their Buddhist cultivation.

Although anyone can practice Buddha-mindfulness, each person does not practice it in the exact same manner owing to individual differences in capacity and knowledge. In the following sections, I will give an overview of five different levels of Buddha-mindfulness. I will begin with the easiest and progress to the most advanced.

Level 1: Reciting Buddha's Name in a Casual Manner

People who recite Buddha's name in a casual, spur of the moment fashion are novice practitioners of Buddha-mindfulness. They do not truly understand why they should take up this Dharma-door, and they may not even be aware of the difference between Buddha-mindfulness and recitation of Buddha's name.

These people have heard about the many benefits of Buddha-mindfulness and decided to begin practicing by chanting Buddha's name aloud. However, when they chant Buddha's name, their minds remain continuously occupied with distracting thoughts stemming from greed, aversion, delusion, arrogance, and doubts. They sometimes attend group practices of Buddha-mindfulness, but they will not go if the weather is bad or if they are not in the mood. In everyday life, they recite Buddha's name silently in their mind when they feel like doing it, but most of the time, their minds are restless and possessed by all sorts of worldly concerns and discursive thoughts.

LEVEL 2: RECITING BUDDHA'S NAME REGULARLY AND CONSISTENTLY

People who recite Buddha's name in a regular and consistent fashion have put down a lot of good roots and performed numerous meritorious deeds in their past lives. Consequently, they are always in the company of those who practice Buddha-mindfulness, and they enjoy guidance from their virtuous companions. These people gradually become aware of the reasons for—and the benefits of—practicing Buddha-mindfulness and develop the ability to recite Buddha's name continuously. Sometimes they can even focus single-mindedly on the Buddha's name, constantly reciting in silence.

Some people may not have taken the initiative to practice Buddha-mindfulness themselves. Rather, they came to the practice via favorable conditions, such as having parents, teachers, or friends who were active participants in group practices of Buddha-mindfulness. When one of these friends or family members passed away, they saw the peaceful, radiant physical appearance of the deceased and were moved by the solemn yet soothing manner of those chanting Buddha's name at the side of the deceased. These personal experiences inspire them to take up Buddha-mindfulness and they begin reciting Buddha's name in silence all the time. Eventually, they will seek to understand the benefits of Buddha-mindfulness, the vows and deeds of the Buddha (or bodhisattva) whose name they recite, and the magnificent attributes of Buddha's pure land.

LEVEL 3: BUDDHA-MINDFULNESS THROUGH NAME RECITATION AND MINDFULNESS

People who can practice Buddha-mindfulness by reciting the Buddha's name while maintaining constant mindfulness of the Buddha are fully aware of the magnificent qualities of Buddha's pure lands (this term is usually used in reference to Sukhāvatī, Buddha Amitābha's Pure Land of Ultimate Bliss). They have strong faith in the existence of the Pure Land of Ultimate Bliss, as well as Buddha Amitābha's forty-eight great vows as told by Buddha Śākyamuni, the World-Honored One. They firmly believe that they can be reborn in the Pure Land of Ultimate Bliss by practicing Buddha-mindfulness, and they vow with utmost sincerity to take rebirth there.

Because they deeply wish to gain rebirth in a pure land, they explore and practice Buddha-mindfulness in depth. They constantly think of the Buddha and contemplate his virtues and merits. Seeking to master Buddha-mindfulness, they spend a great deal of time practicing this method, as well as reading the writings on Buddha-mindfulness composed by virtuous and knowledgeable teachers.

Through these efforts, they will eventually come to recognize the distinction between the recitation of Buddha's name and the Dharma-door of Buddha-mindfulness. Also, they will arrive at the understanding that during practice, they should not only chant Buddha's name, but should accompany their chanting with mental recitation; not only perform mental recitation but also listen to this mental recitation in their minds; not only listen to this mental recitation, but also be mindful of the Buddha at the same time; and not only be mindful of the Buddha, but also maintain their mindfulness in a continuous manner, such that eventually they can subdue all distracting thoughts and carry on the name recitation and the mindfulness without interruption.

This method—recitation of Buddha's name in conjunction with continuous mindfulness of Buddha—should be practiced regularly on a weekly or daily basis. During group practice, you should not chant with too loud a voice or else it may affect your energy flow or health. The key is to hold the thought of Buddha in mind while reciting Buddha's name. As the recitation becomes unbroken, the thought of Buddha continues without interruption. When the mind becomes dull or when you cannot keep up the recitation, you should resume your chanting of Buddha's name with the group in a voice that is neither too loud nor too low and maintain mindfulness of Buddha at the same time. During the rest of the day, you should recite Buddha's name silently and practice mental recitation along with mental listening.

When you can distinguish the mental recitation and mental listening that go on in your mind with distinct clarity, you can replace the mental listening with mindfulness. During mental recitation and mental listening, you chant Buddha's name silently while listening to the sounds of Buddha's name with one-pointed focus to make sure that the silent recitation goes on uninterruptedly. Not many people can achieve this level of meditative concentration (*samādhi*).

When the silent recitation and mental listening go on in your mind are clear and continuous, you are ready to take a step forward and explore the purpose of mental recitation and mental listening. With careful contemplation and investigation, you will see that the purpose of coupling mental recitation with mental listening is to dispel wandering thoughts by keeping the mind in a state of mental absorption. The thought of Buddha during this practice is looming and not very clear; sometimes, when the mind enters a state of deep absorption, it is totally absent.

Once you can observe your mental state with such clarity, you will know that it is time to adjust your method. Rather than listening to the mental recitation of Buddha's name, now you should accompany the mental recitation with mindfulness. In other words, you are mentally reciting the Buddha's name while maintaining in mind a continuous pure thought of Buddha without interruption.

By the time you reach this stage in your cultivation, you will probably have obtained a vision of the Buddha or bodhisattva of which you are mindful, or have received some responsive sign from him. This will greatly enhance your confidence in the practice, and in turn, it will make you less likely to backslide from your achievement.

LEVEL 4: SIGNLESS BUDDHA-MINDFULNESS

If you are one of those practitioners who can reach the stage of signless mindfulness of Buddha, you must have, in past lives, paid homage and made offerings to the World-Honored One and the Three Jewels, cultivated uncountable good roots and merits, and diligently cultivated meditative concentration and the Pure Land methods with equal emphasis. In addition, you must have often sought the company of virtuous and knowledgeable mentors without blindly following the teachings you received, and you must have earnestly explored and reflected upon the Dharma-door of Buddha-mindfulness in order to steadily improve your practice. Even though in this present life the Dharma-door of Buddha-mindfulness is the primary method of your Dharma cultivation, you do not neglect to acquire knowledge of meditative concentration. Having acquired fundamental knowledge of the practices of both the Pure Land tradition and of meditative concentration, you will, in the course of diligent and continuous learning and cultivation, naturally reach the level of signless mindfulness—the ability to sustain in your mind a bare thought of Buddha that is free of Buddha's name or appearance. Equipped with abundant good roots, merits and knowledge, you know without a doubt that this signless mindfulness of Buddha is the true way to practice Buddha-mindfulness and therefore you endeavor to continue in this method resolutely. As well, you have full confidence that you will be reborn into a higher level and grade in the Pure Land of Ultimate Bliss.

In the section "Bodhisattva Mahāsthāmaprāpta's Dharma-Door for Perfect Mastery through Buddha-Mindfulness" of the *Śūraṅgama Sūtra*, Bodhisattva Mahāsthāmaprāpta describes his select method of Buddha-mindfulness with the words "recollect and be mindful of Buddha" as well as "rein in the six sense faculties and abide in one continuous pure thought." Signless mindfulness of Buddha is precisely this Dharma-door taught by Bodhisattva Mahāsthāmaprāpta. If consistent practice of signless Buddha-mindfulness is combined with slow prostrations to Buddha, you can easily develop the skill to maintain signless mindfulness throughout any activity of everyday life, regardless of whether you are in motion or in stillness.

When you have mastered signless mindfulness of Buddha and can maintain it throughout your daily activities, you will have full confidence in the Three Jewels as well as in your own capacity to master the Dharma-door of Buddha-mindfulness. You will never abandon the Three Jewels in your present life. Also, the thought of transcending the three realms of existence will naturally arise in your mind. During personal or group practices, if you are able to recite Buddha's name attentively and maintain Buddha mindfulness until there is no more name to recite—when no name arises and yet your mind is still focused upon the Buddha one-pointedly and continuously—you will comprehend experientially what is meant by the words "abiding in one continuous pure thought."

If you apply yourself ever diligently, entering deep into mindfulness, contemplation, and practice, you will eventually arrive at this insight: the image of the Buddha, his sacred name, or the sound of his sacred name—none of these is the Buddha; even a vision of the Buddha is not the Buddha. The word "buddha" means the enlightened one, which is none other than the one Mind. Buddha Śākyamuni, who lived in India 2,500 years ago, was only a response-body manifested by his Dharma-body (*dharmakāya*). The ultimate origin of the Buddha is without birth and death. This true "Buddha" is neither existence nor emptiness, yet not apart from existence or emptiness—it is none other than one's True Mind. The Buddha we are mindful of is essentially this True Mind, which is inherently without name, sound, or form. If this is the Mind we are mindful of when we recollect the Buddha, why would we need to employ names, sounds, or forms during our practice to sustain the mindfulness? When you thoroughly understand this truth through your own reasoning and contemplation, you will be able to relinquish the use of names, sounds, and forms in your practice and advance to the stage of signless mindfulness of Buddha.

Moreover, if you can bring this pure thought of Buddha from a sitting practice into your everyday activities, you will see the results of preliminary accomplishment in signless Buddha-mindfulness within one to three days. If you practice very diligently and experience it in depth, within one or two months, or even one or two weeks, you will be able to remain in constant mindfulness of Buddha effortlessly and spontaneously: the thought of Buddha will pour into your mind like a gushing spring and will be present naturally without any willful effort.

Although your mindfulness of Buddha at this stage is free of any sign, you are mindful of one particular Buddha only and not all the Buddhas of ten directions. And in spite of the signlessness of the thought of Buddha, you know very clearly which Buddha is the object of your mindfulness. This signless bare thought of Buddha is difficult to understand for most people, but those who are skilled in the recitation of Buddha's name should find it easier to comprehend. To help practitioners reach the stage of signless mindfulness quickly, I have devised a slow prostration practice to Buddha to augment the practice of signless mindfulness. For details, please refer to my book *Signless Buddha-Mindfulness.*

The cultivation of signless Buddha-mindfulness requires one to reduce, or preferably eliminate, skeptical doubts, arrogance, and the mind's habitual tendencies of clinging and grasping, perceiving and observing. The tendency of the mind to cling to and grasp at sensory objects makes it difficult to give up the use of names, sounds, and forms. Even if you can let go of these signs, you will still find it challenging to hold in mind a continuous pure thought of Buddha. The tendencies to perceive and observe sensory objects cause mental restlessness and skeptical doubts. If not abandoned, you will constantly be on the lookout for responsive signs from Buddhas or bodhisattvas, making it difficult for you to settle into a state of signless mindfulness and hold on to the pure thought of Buddha.

If skeptical doubt about this practice persists, you might consider signless Buddha-mindfulness to be groundless and question whether it is a real Buddhist practice, or you may be wary of trying this Dharma-door until it becomes widely accepted after perhaps ten, twenty, fifty, or even a hundred years. It would be a shame if, by that time, you are too old to practice or have passed on to your next life, uncertain of the possibility of encountering this wonderful Dharma-door again.

As a matter of fact, quite a few ancient and contemporary Dharma masters have discussed this particular Dharma-door of Buddha-mindfulness. However, in this Dharma-ending age, those who circulate Buddhist publications often neglect to propagate this practice because many believe that the mental state of signless mindfulness is too difficult to achieve. On the other hand, a few individuals conveniently interpret the recollection and mindfulness of Buddha taught by many great masters of the past as simply the recitation of Buddha's name. Consequently, practitioners of Buddha-mindfulness are confused and hesitant to place their trust in this method.

Another type of person finds it hard to practice Buddha-mindfulness: those plagued by arrogance. Some people consider Chan practice to be superior. Even when they cannot figure out what a *huatou* is after trying for ten or twenty years, they remain steadfast and simply will not give up on it. These people merit both respect and pity. Another type of arrogant person is the one who buries himself in exhaustive studies of Buddhist scriptures in order to become a renowned scholar. But time flies and old age soon comes upon them. These two types of people usually do not want to stoop to the practice of Buddha-mindfulness or be in the company of those who practice Buddha-mindfulness.

The lotus flower is an icon in Buddhism for a very good reason. While the lotus flower symbolizes the purity and dignity of the Buddha Dharma, it grows out of the lowly mud in a pond. By analogy, the abandonment of arrogance and the embracing of humility will bring about swift mastery of the Dharma and the practice of Buddha-mindfulness.

I have been teaching the Buddha Dharma through the Dharma-door of Buddha-mindfulness since May 1989 and have seen firsthand that arrogance can hurt Buddhist learners with a magnitude that is deep and broad. Humble people progress quickly in their cultivation, whereas arrogant individuals tend to worship authority figures and cannot believe that a virtuous, knowledgeable mentor is not necessarily famous. Even if a virtuous, knowledgeable mentor appears before them, they will not have faith in him or her and hence will miss the chance to learn. Therefore, the elimination of an arrogant mentality is crucial if you want to enter deep into the Dharma-door of Buddha-mindfulness.

Progressing from Phenomena-Based to Principle-Based Practice: The Ordinary Mind Is Not Apart from the Buddha Mind

While this practice is called signless Buddha-mindfulness, the mental state achieved through this practice is not the ultimate reality. This method is called "signless" to highlight its dispensing with worldly characteristics, such as names, sounds, images, and the like.

Moreover, although the ultimate reality is without signs, the absence of signs is not necessarily the ultimate reality. The word *signless* in "signless Buddha-mindfulness refers to the absence of signs and characteristics that can be understood within the limits of our worldly comprehension, as in the signlessness of signless Buddha-mindfulness, the pristine and thoughtless awareness, the sentient beings residing in the formless realm, the infinite space, and so forth. Ultimate reality, on the contrary, is beyond all worldly comprehensions and conceptualizations; the true suchness, Buddha-nature, *bodhi*, and nirvana all fall into this category.

In Mahāyāna Buddhism, the ultimate reality does not mean only the absence of worldly signs. It is also defined by the non-duality of emptiness and existence. The ultimate reality is not sign and yet not apart from sign; it is without sign but is not non-sign; it is neither emptiness nor existence, and yet not separated from either. Thus, it is called the "Middle Way." Given that the realization of this transcendental truth is not even comprehensible for those who have realized the True Mind but have not yet seen the Buddha-nature, how is it possible for an ordinary person to understand it using the mental consciousness' faculties of reasoning and contemplation?

While the mental state of signless Buddha-mindfulness is not the ultimate reality, this mental state nevertheless does exist and has been documented since ancient times. To propagate the Dharma-door of Buddha-mindfulness for the benefits of practitioners of both the Chan and Pure Land traditions in this Dharma-ending age, I have named this practice "signless Buddha-mindfulness" based on the following passage from Vol. 4 of *The Great Jewel Heap Sūtra* (*Mahāratnakūṭa Sūtra*):

> Signlessness refers to the absence of an individual body and its designations, as well as words, sentences, and appearances.

It must be noted that signless Buddha-mindfulness, in spite of its desertion of signs and characteristics, is merely a method of Buddha-mindfulness practiced on the causal ground. Upon successful mastery of this method of Buddha-mindfulness, you will find that the signless thought of Buddha fills your mind unremittingly like a gushing spring. The Dharma-joy this experience generates will fade away and finally disappear with the passage of time as you get used to it. If you continue to practice signless Buddha-mindfulness, sooner or later you will be abruptly seized by an introspective question: "*Who* is bearing Buddha in mind?" Or you may be swept off your feet, lose all sense of direction, and drop into a dark barrel the moment a virtuous, knowledgeable mentor suddenly throws at you the question, "*Who* is bearing Buddha in mind?" Hereafter you will be consumed each and every moment by an intense doubt, as if you have a delicious but steaming hot dumpling stuck in your mouth; you cannot swallow it but nor do you want to spit it out.

Now you will have to call upon your solid skill of signless Buddha-mindfulness to thoroughly probe into this doubt without using language, a process known as "Buddha-mindfulness through experiential investigation." One day the realization will transpire: the physical body, its perceptions and sensations, the illusory mind and the consciousnesses, none of them are *me*. The real *me* is the Mind that never had a single thought. Right there and right then you confirm your realization without hesitation. Henceforth, you will be acquainted with the origin and the source of all sentient existences and can directly comprehend the invisible True Mind. Never again will you mistake the thoughtless and pristine awareness for the True Mind.

Upon awakening to the True Mind, some burst out into cackles, some weep in rapture, and still others remain inscrutable, settling calmly into the state of the True Mind. In any case, you will suddenly experience a lightened feeling that your body and mind have turned lucid and pure.

The realization of the True Mind entails the simultaneous elimination of the view of self (*ātmadṛṣṭi*), which in turn casts out all skeptical doubts about the ultimate reality and all misconceptions about disciplines and precepts. Upon severing these "three fetters," your practice of signless Buddha-mindfulness becomes Buddha-mindfulness of the fruition ground. However, at this stage, you are only considered to be a stream-enterer (*srotâpanna*) heading toward the noble fruitions and are not a real noble person yet. This is because, at this stage, you have not entered the ultimate reality by seeing with the naked eye your Buddha-nature but have only found the True Mind. In consequence, you will regard emptiness, one end of the two extremes, as the ultimate reality. Your next cultivation target is to see the Buddha-nature so that you can advance to the stage of Buddha-mindfulness in ultimate reality.

LEVEL 5: BUDDHA-MINDFULNESS IN ULTIMATE REALITY

Not many practitioners of Buddha-mindfulness are able to master signless Buddha-mindfulness, and it is even rarer for one to uncover the True Mind and cut off the three fetters with the aid of signless Buddha-mindfulness and Buddha-mindfulness through experiential investigation. Lamentably though, most of the time, the realization of the True Mind marks the end of the cultivation for those practitioners who do reach this point. After the practitioner receives validation of his awakening, he is usually advised by his master to maintain this realization by continued practice of Buddha-mindfulness through experiential investigation, and no further teaching and cultivation take place beyond this point. Time and resources are squandered in idleness as the practitioner does not know that he should work toward seeing the Buddha-nature by means of Buddha-mindfulness through experiential investigation.

If you are practicing Buddha-mindfulness on the fruition ground and are aware of this fact, you should drop all worldly engagements to seek a virtuous, knowledgeable mentor (maybe different from the one who helped you attain awakening to the True Mind) who can help you further your cultivation. When you come across such a mentor, after verifying your realization and examining your capacity, he or she may give you a slap, fling you an apple, or wave a fist right in front of your eyes. If none of these tricks suffice to induce you to see the Buddha-nature, the mentor may assign one or two Dharma sayings for you to ponder over.

If you strive earnestly to contemplate the answer by way of Buddha-mindfulness through experiential investigation, then it is only a matter of time before you stumble upon your Buddha-nature. It could be the feeling of hot or cold, a fall to the ground, the barking of a dog, the colorful sight of flowers and leaves, the feeling of joy or sadness, or anything around you that prompts you to see your Buddha-nature in one corresponding thought, upon which another part of ignorance will be removed. You will then come to realize the pervasiveness of your

Buddha-nature. A grin will spread across your face and you cannot help but laugh at your own stupidity—the Buddha-nature has always been right under your nose, yet you were never aware of it. You can't help but start looking around, touching and feeling everything in sight to experience its pervasive existence.

Alternatively, you may come to this breakthrough while carrying out experiential investigation during sitting meditation. After realizing the Buddha-nature in one corresponding moment, you will follow all of the surrounding sounds to thoroughly experience its ubiquity. Even when the meditation is over, you will continue to experience its presence everywhere.

Once you have seen the Buddha-nature with your naked eye, you will understand what is meant by the dual practice of Chan and Pure Land and why the two traditions are said to be interconnected. You dwell single-mindedly in a luminous awareness, without discursive thoughts, language, parameters, or worldly conceptualizations. Beyond description, the essence of such a state can only be captured by the word "awakening." This is actually the state of "one-pointed absorption within principle," wherein one directly perceives the origin, or the Dharma-body, of all Buddhas. Hereafter, for seven or maybe seventy consecutive days, you dwell in a luminous awareness, unaffected by drowsiness and distractions. Deluded thoughts do not arise and no thoughts can take your focus away. Instead, you observe the absolute emptiness and true existence of the Buddha-nature in all sense-objects—forms, sounds, odors, tastes, tactile and mental objects—as well as how it gives rise to all phenomena. At night, you may not feel sleepy and may lie in bed with a lucid mind until dawn; or you may wake up at three or four o'clock in the morning fully refreshed, rise, wash up, offer incense, prostrate to Buddha, and then say to yourself, "Actually, I have never ever prostrated to Buddha!"

From then on, the body, mind, and physical world have all lost their realness. When you read the sutras that expound the ultimate truth, you find the words close to heart, as if they are all describing the workings of your own mind. But if you tell others about your observations and experiences, they might think you are just repeating the teachings on the profound ultimate truth and may teasingly say, "You have to get beyond the terminology and do more real practice." Hearing this, you don't know whether to laugh or cry. Actually, you will derive many more functional benefits from the seeing of Buddha-nature. I will not get into these benefits in this book; you will discover them yourself when you reach this stage.

SPONTANEOUS AWAKENING TO THE TRUE MIND WITHOUT EMPLOYING SKILLFUL MEANS

What I have described in the previous sections are the stages that most people go through to reach Buddha-mindfulness through experiential investigation, or what is called "principle-based Buddha-mindfulness." While in the previous section the realization of the True Mind and the seeing of the Buddha-nature are presented as two separate, successive events, it needs to be pointed out that an individual with superior capacity is able to realize the True Mind and see the Buddha-nature (the Dharma-body of Buddha) at the same time and without the help of a knowledgeable mentor.

The section "Bodhisattva Mahāsthāmaprāpta's Dharma-door for Perfect Mastery through Buddha-Mindfulness" in the *Śūraṅgama Sūtra* states, "If sentient beings recollect and are mindful of Buddha, certainly they will see the Buddha now or in the future." "In the future" means that one will surely see the Buddha in a future lifetime when one reaches the state of one-pointed absorption within principle. The "Buddha" that one will see does not refer to a vision of a Buddha's embodiment but to one's own intrinsic Buddha—the Dharma-body of all Buddhas and all sentient beings—upon which a person will suddenly become awakened and think, "I never would have thought that *this* is the Dharma-body of all Buddhas and the 'original face' of all sentient beings." If this practitioner of Buddha-mindfulness has practiced Chan contemplation before, he would also remark, "Knowing the spot where the monk of Tucheng (referring to the Venerable Guang Qin [1892–1986] of Tucheng, Taiwan) once stood, I could have given it thirty good cane strokes."

The entire process of achieving Buddha-mindfulness in ultimate reality, from the emergence of the "sense of doubt" until the moment of seeing Buddha-nature, demonstrates how one's mind "will spontaneously awaken to the True Mind without employing skillful means." Why is no expedient method necessary to facilitate this process? Because the mental state in signless Buddha-mindfulness corresponds extremely well with the signless nature of the ultimate reality, allowing you to cultivate Chan without having to learn it, to contemplate *huatou* without having to study it, to bring up the sense of doubt spontaneously without going through head-breaking struggles, and eventually, to open the mind without the aid of a knowledgeable mentor. The entire process of awakening to the True Mind may take as little as one day or as long as ten years; some will even have to wait until the next lifetime. Hence the statement: "certainly they will see the Buddha now or in the future." In other words, your mind will certainly be awakened; it is just a matter of time.

Once your mind is awakened and you gain direct comprehension of the Buddha-nature, any methods of Buddha-mindfulness you practice—be it oral recitation, visualization, or signless mindfulness—is essentially Buddha-mindfulness in ultimate reality. Why? Because the ultimate reality is apart from yet exists together with all worldly characteristics. It is neither emptiness nor existence, and at the same time it is both emptiness and existence. At this stage, insofar as you have thoroughly understood and mastered the practice and principle of Buddha-mindfulness and can teach others how to go about it, you are qualified to say, "One recitation of the Buddha's name encompasses both phenomena and principle."

Your practice at this stage has taken on an entirely different dimension than before your mind was awakened. Now you are mindful of Buddha with the Mind, that is, you are thinking of Buddha's True Mind with your own True Mind. The mind that recollects and the mind being recollected are the same. [Note: Although the mind that can recollect is illusory, it is nevertheless produced by the True Mind and is, therefore, one of its attributes. Therefore, to an enlightened person, the one that recollects and the one being recollected are not two separate entities.] The difference between you and Buddha is that Buddha has perfected his cultivation of wisdom, meditative concentration, and merits but you have not. Looking ahead, while you will never again fall back into the three evil paths, there is still a long way to go before you can attain Buddhahood—an understanding that humbles you when you think about the Buddha in your practice. Thinking about other Buddhists who have not reached this level, compassion and sympathy will fill your heart and motivate you to dedicate yourself to helping them achieve what you have.

When you have reached the level of Buddha-mindfulness in ultimate reality, you will be received by Buddha Amitābha at the end of your life and will be born in the highest level of the highest grade in the Pure Land of Ultimate Bliss. You will also receive a comforting sign before you pass away. Immediately after dying, you will be taken to the pure land on a diamond platform and attain the acquiescence to the non-arising of dharma (*anutpattikadharmakṣānti*) upon seeing Buddha Amitābha. In the Pure Land of Ultimate Bliss, you can travel in an instant to all Buddha lands in ten directions to pay homage and make offerings to innumerable Buddhas. After you have received predictions for Buddhahood from all the Buddhas, you will return to the Pure Land of Ultimate Bliss and acquire the great Dharma-door of total retention of uncountable *dhāraṇīs*.

By now, you will have acquired from your cultivation many tremendously beneficial and meritorious qualities of liberation. For instance, if you are insulted in public, you can simply ignore it and no anger or animosity will develop in your mind. Nevertheless, you should not become complacent because of this accomplishment. In addition to assisting other learners to practice Buddha-mindfulness, you should continue to cultivate Buddha-mindfulness in a broad sense. The main focus of your cultivation now should be the knowledge-of-the-aspects-of-paths (*mārgajñatā*) and the four basic levels of meditative concentration (the four *dhyānas*). A notable advantage of having entered the ultimate reality and eradicated most afflictions is that the progress of your cultivation of meditative concentration will be tens or thousands of times faster than that of those who have not. Once you have attained the four concentrations, you should practice the contemplation, forging, refining and mastery of meditative concentration, which will subsequently bring about immeasurable *samādhis* over the course of your cultivation along the bodhisattva path, equipping you with the ability to benefit uncountable sentient beings. In conclusion, you should not be satisfied with just the level of Buddha-mindfulness in ultimate reality but should further your cultivation of the Buddha Dharma.

CLEARING UP DOUBTS

Some people might say, "This article is about Buddha-mindfulness, so it should not be talking about Chan." This article actually focuses on the adjustments you need to make so that you can make advancement in your practice of Buddha-mindfulness.

Most people who practice Buddha-mindfulness by reciting Buddha's name remain at the stage of mental recitation in conjunction with mental listening, not knowing that they should move on to practice mental recitation in conjunction with constant mindfulness. Some practitioners have reached the level of concurrent mental recitation and mindfulness but do not know that they can leave behind all characteristics and signs and progress to signless mindfulness. Others are even troubled when the Buddha's name no longer comes forth during their practice, or do not know that the continuous presence of the thought of Buddha in their minds is an indication that they are ready to move on to Buddha-mindfulness through experiential investigation, an adjustment that marks the leap from phenomena-based to principle-based practice. I have also seen practitioners who are held up at the level of signless Buddha-mindfulness due to insufficient knowledge or a rejection of Chan. As a result, they cannot advance from signless mindfulness to Buddha-mindfulness in ultimate reality, thus missing the chance of "seeing the Buddha" and, consequently, the chance to be born in the highest grade and level in the Pure Land of Ultimate Bliss. All these problems stem from deficient understanding about making appropriate adjustments in the practice of Buddha-mindfulness.

Although there are eighty-four thousand Dharma-doors of liberation in the Buddha Dharma, the cultivation of each Dharma-door must eventually correspond with the ultimate truth (i.e., the ultimate reality). Be it the tranquility and insight meditation (*samathavipaśyanā*) practice of the Tiantai school, the Chan contemplation of the Chan school, Buddha-mindfulness of the Pure

Land school, or any other Dharma-door, the final stage of cultivation leading up to the direct comprehension of the ultimate truth is all Chan in essence.

Moreover, during the course of cultivating any Dharma-door, some adjustments are always necessary to train a distracted mind into a focused one. Once you have developed sufficient power of meditative concentration, you can then begin to investigate and seek the True Mind and eventually directly comprehend its nature of emptiness—an achievement known as the awakening to the True Mind. After this direct perception of the True Mind, described in the scripture as "seeing that which is without seeing," you can continue to contemplate and investigate experientially until you see the Buddha-nature with your naked eye. The direct comprehension of the ultimate reality by seeing the Buddha-nature brings forth the insights that can be used to teach and guide other practitioners.

The adjustments you have to make in your practice take different forms and manners depending on which cultivation method you adopt. Nevertheless, the underlying principle is the same. In other words, Chan is not exclusive to the Chan school but is present in all Dharma-doors of liberation. The protracted course of cultivation in all Dharma-doors that precedes the final stage of liberation is invariably for the building up of your knowledge and power of meditative concentration. Only when both are adequate will you know when and how to make appropriate adjustments—then Chan will show itself when conditions mature.

"Restrain the mind to observe the precepts, adhere to precepts to produce concentration, employ concentration to develop insights": this is a condensed summary of the way to liberation. The general principle underlying the adjustments required in any Dharma-door is to move from the use of signs to their abandonment, and then employ signlessness as an expedient means to enter the ultimate reality. Once the ultimate reality is realized, there is no differentiation between the presence of signs and signlessness. Hence, the Tiantai school claims that "The principle and the phenomena are not two"; the Chan school says that "The mountain hues are nothing but the pure body, the babbling of the brook is the vast, long tongue of the Buddha"; and the Pure Land school states that "One recitation of the Buddha's name encompasses both phenomena and principle."

The principles and guidelines for making adjustments in Buddha-mindfulness in fact apply to the practices of any Buddhist school or tradition. In one scripture, the Buddha mentions that to the east of our Sahā world there is a world called Animiṣo (unblinking) where linguistic expressions do not exist. However, the Buddha of that world can still teach the Dharma to bodhisattvas. Likewise, a practitioner of signless Buddha-mindfulness does not tie the thought of Buddha to linguistic forms or the sounds of recitation. He gradually improves and fine tunes his practice until he can contemplate *huatou* and advance to Buddha-mindfulness through experiential investigation, until he can finally attain direct perception of the dharma-realm (*dharmadhātu*), i.e., the reality of all phenomena. I will cite a passage from Vol. 4 of the *Sūtra on the Mahāyāna Path to the Six Pāramitās* to illustrate my point:

> At that time, the Bhagavān said to long-lived Ānanda again, "The world of Animiṣo has no suffering and the three evil paths are unheard of [...] its land is magnificent and pure, where only Buddha, the lord of Dharma, teaches Dharma to all bodhisattvas without the use of written or spoken language. When bodhisattvas come to see the Buddha, they join their palms together in reverence, fix their eyes intently and steadily on the Buddha, and attain the Buddha-Mindfulness

Samādhi. Thus this world is called Animiṣo. What is the Buddha-Mindfulness Samādhi? The Buddha-Mindfulness Samādhi is attained neither through forms, nor through sensation, perception, formation, or consciousness, nor through the insights of the limits of past or future, nor from what one sees and hears at the moment." The Buddha told Ānanda, "This Buddha-Mindfulness Samādhi is inconceivable. It does not act on any dharma, yet it comprehends the suchness and ultimate reality of all dharmas. It is without speech, manifestation, sign, or name—such is called the Buddha-Mindfulness Samādhi."

In the above passage, the world of Animiṣo, as described by the World-Honored One, has neither written nor spoken language. When the bodhisattvas in that world visit their Buddha and receive his teachings, as long as they respectfully join their palms and behold the Buddha with an intent and fixed gaze, they will effortlessly attain the Buddha-Mindfulness Samādhi and immediately realize the wordless and speechless "intrinsic Buddha." In short, they enter the ultimate reality directly through the expedient of signlessness.

Why do the bodhisattvas in this world not have to go through the various levels of Buddha-mindfulness, starting with name recitation, before attaining the Buddha-Mindfulness Samādhi? Buddha-mindfulness through experiential investigation refers to the process through which one carries out mental investigation for the purpose of realizing the ultimate reality. The aim of Buddha-mindfulness is invariably to see the real Buddha—the reality of all phenomena known as the dharma-realm. This is what the words "seeing the Buddha" really mean. Why is this the true meaning of "seeing the Buddha"? The World-Honored One makes it very clear that the Buddha-Mindfulness Samādhi cannot be attained through the dharma characteristics of form, sensation, perception, formation, or consciousness, nor can it be achieved through the insights derived from the twelve links of dependent arising, or the perceptual faculties of seeing, hearing, feeling, and knowing that we experience here and now.

The Buddha-Mindfulness Samādhi is beyond the imagination and comprehension of a person's mental consciousness. The intrinsic Buddha is inherently without the perceptive faculties of seeing, hearing, feeling, and knowing. When you realize the intrinsic Buddha in one corresponding thought, you will be able to observe with *prajñā* (wisdom regarding the True Mind) that it is the origin of all dharmas of the five aggregates; that the intrinsic Buddha itself, the seeds of the five aggregates that it stores, and the myriad meritorious qualities it possesses are all uncreated; and that the intrinsic Buddha gives rise to the five aggregates in dependence on specific conditions. Such are the true realities of all phenomena. Thus, the intrinsic Buddha is called the ultimate reality of all phenomena, and the insight with which one can directly comprehend these realities is termed the Buddha-Mindfulness Samādhi. With this insight, you can swiftly enter the Way, as you would be able to make correct choices during your cultivation of the various Dharma-doors of liberation.

SINCERE REMINDER

To experience the benefits of Buddha-mindfulness, a beginner of this Dharma-door should participate regularly in group practices and study the works of virtuous and knowledgeable mentors to augment his or her personal practice of Buddha-mindfulness through recitation. During the course of diligent cultivation toward the stage of signless Buddha-mindfulness, you might encounter extraordinary signs, such as seeing light, smelling fragrance, obtaining visions of a golden image of the Buddha, and so forth. Albeit delightful and encouraging, you should not become attached to them. On rare occasions (less than one out of ten thousand), you might even see the Buddha speaking the Dharma to you during meditation. If that happens, you must verify all teachings you heard with the Three Dharma Seals (*dharmamudrā*) and the Four Reliances (*pratisaraṇa*) before following them. Some people may experience ease and composure, coolness, the feeling of joyfulness and compassion, dwindling of arrogance, or entering into a state of mental absorption after they have mastered signless Buddha-mindfulness. These are all signs of entering into a state of mental absorption, so you need not be alarmed but should continue to deepen your practice.

In recent years, I have come across a few Buddhist learners who were able to enter, by way of Chan contemplation or Buddha-mindfulness through experiential investigation, a mental state empty of language and deluded thoughts. Not knowing that what they have achieved is merely a mental state of the illusory mind, they regarded this signless mental state of Buddha-mindfulness as the "true self" (True Mind). They reported this achievement to their masters and obtained certification of enlightenment. The problem is, if this mental state void of language and deluded thoughts were indeed the True Mind, then the minds of all wordless and thoughtless animals as well as the pristine awareness attained via meditative concentration should be the True Mind as well. So why are those animals and those who abide in pristine awareness not enjoying the virtues and benefits of liberation?

The subtle distinctions between true versus false enlightenment can only be discerned by an enlightened teacher, who can impart right views and lead practitioners to the right paths. The pristine awareness is not the True Mind in spite of its thoughtlessness; nor is the seeing of flowers (projected by the illusory mind) during meditation a sign of realization. Such misconceptions, if not clarified, will blind you from realizing the True Mind's nature of emptiness, and it will be impossible for you to enter the ultimate reality, a state of non-duality of emptiness and existence.

For the reasons above, the guidance of a virtuous and knowledgeable mentor is paramount when a practitioner is entering the level of Buddha-mindfulness through experiential investigation. A virtuous and knowledgeable mentor is one who has already advanced into the level of Buddha-mindfulness in ultimate reality himself. He can see the Buddha-nature without retrogressing from this realization, is proficient in the understanding of the ultimate truth, and possesses skillful means to teach others how to proceed from sign-dependent to signless mindfulness of Buddha and then how to use signless mindfulness as an expedient means to enter the ultimate reality. One must keep in mind that such a mentor is not necessarily well known. But famous or not, he can show the practitioners the proper way to cultivate Buddha-mindfulness and verify their realization. He will ensure that they do not mistake the illusory mind for the True Mind, or the false enlightenment for true enlightenment. He is able to lead practitioners to the level of Buddha-mindfulness in ultimate reality through the right stages and help them abandon obsessions with exotic experiences that take place during meditation.

Fortunately, it is not difficult to find such virtuous, knowledgeable mentors in Taiwan as their number is on the rise. That being said, it is more important for a practitioner of Buddha-mindfulness to establish faith and confidence, subdue arrogance, bring forth the aspiration for Buddhahood (*bodhicitta*), and practice the bodhisattva's way of life. Without these qualities, you would not recognize a virtuous, knowledgeable mentor even if he were standing right in front of you.

In this book, I have discussed five levels of Buddha-mindfulness that can bring practitioners to reach phenomena-based and principle-based practice of Buddha-mindfulness. Though mastering signless Buddha-mindfulness is not an easy task, it is not as difficult as it seems if you commit yourself to it with diligence, employ skillful means, and progress in the right steps. As for Buddha-mindfulness in ultimate reality, while it is difficult to attain for most people, it is not a stage entirely impossible to reach. If after having attained the Samādhi of Signless Buddha-Mindfulness, you are able to constantly abide in mindfulness, rid yourself of arrogance, bring forth the aspiration for enlightenment, and pray to the Buddha on your knees to guide you to a virtuous, knowledgeable teacher, you will surely meet the right teacher who may bring you to an awakening with only a few words. If you have not yet found a virtuous, knowledgeable teacher, it means that causes and conditions have not matured yet. Do not be discouraged. Continue your practice of Buddha-mindfulness through experiential investigation with thoroughness. Even if you cannot see the Buddha-nature in this life, you will be able to in the future as long as you do not fall into the three evil destinies.

If you have the disposition of a bodhisattva, after you have mastered signless Buddha-mindfulness, you might be able to personally realize the ultimate reality after two or three years of self-cultivation and verify your realization with multiple scriptures and treatises. Please be advised that it is not possible to seek the ultimate reality through Buddha-mindfulness if you do not bring forth the magnanimous mind of a bodhisattva and remove arrogance and timidity.

Lastly, I would like to extend my heartfelt encouragement to all Buddhist learners through this prayer: May all Buddhist disciples engage in the practice of Buddha-mindfulness, recollecting and being mindful of Buddha, such that all will see the Buddha now or in the future, and benefit sentient beings with a magnanimous heart.

Holder of the Bodhisattva Precepts
Xiao Pingshi

《如何契入念佛法門》

都攝六根　淨念相繼

　　念佛是三根普被、利鈍兼修的修行法門。尤其適合繁忙緊張生活的現代人。念佛法門簡單易學，八十老翁念得，三歲孩兒也念得；大學教授念得，販夫走卒及不識一字的阿公阿婆也念得。但能信心具足，皆可依其根機而獲得或多或少的利益和感應；若能深入佛法、細意思惟，乃至能因念佛法門而明心見性。有極少數人因為自視為利根人，不屑於念佛，而喪失修行上的大利益，頗令人惋惜感慨。

　　念佛雖然人人念得，卻因根器及知見之不同而有不同之層次。茲將持名念佛法門所修之境界，由淺至深，簡略分述於後：

　　一、隨興持名：此種人剛開始學習念佛法門，還不明白為什麼要念佛！甚至不知道「念」佛與「唸」佛之不同。只是聽說念佛好，便跟著別人學念佛，從持唸佛名開始。口中雖在唸佛號，心中卻老是在打妄想。貪瞋癡慢疑，樣樣皆不離。偶爾參加念佛共修，遇到刮風下雨或心情不佳，便不參加共修。平常心中默持佛號，也只是隨興默唸，大約是打妄想的時候多。

二、唸佛不輟：此種人因為過去生所種善根福德為因，今生復有善侶提攜接引為緣，常與念佛人伴黨；漸漸知悉為什麼要念佛，以及念佛有何好處，已能相續執持佛號。有時可以全心放在佛號上，時時默唱佛號。

亦有人不曾念佛，緣因父母師友平日常與念佛人共修念佛法門，一朝忽然見其捨棄報身，諸蓮友們為其助念佛號，此人賭其父母師友往生時之瑞相，或見念佛人助念時之莊嚴自在，而接受念佛修行法門，時時默唱佛號。也開始瞭解所念之佛菩薩，其本願與事蹟及其佛土世界之依正莊嚴，開始解知念佛之好處。

三、持名憶佛：此人不但已知諸佛土（通常是指極樂世界淨土）之依正莊嚴，深信有極樂世界，深信　釋迦世尊所說彌陀四十八大願絕對真實，深信念佛可以往生彼國，而於深心之中發起誓願，願生彼國。因此開始探索念佛法門，欲求一心深入，時時繫念思惟，漸漸深入研讀善知識們闡述念佛法門之著作，了知唸佛號與念佛之差別。明白了知念佛共修時不但要口唸，還要心唸；不但要心唸，還要心聽；不但要心聽，還要憶念；不但要憶念，還要持續不斷、放下萬緣，不讓妄想打斷佛號與憶念。

如此每週或者每日精進地持唸佛號，配合憶念而不間斷。此種共修念佛，不可大聲唸佛號，以免傷氣傷身。要點在於保持憶佛之念不離佛號；以佛號不斷故，憶佛之念亦不斷。若因昏沉或妄想減少時，即應隨眾不高吭不低沉地持唸佛號，同時憶念於佛。平時則於心中默唱佛號，心念心聽。

若得心念心聽、清楚分明，即應改為心念心憶，以默唸佛號配合憶佛。心念心聽是心中默默念佛號，並專注一心，觀照心中佛號之音聲，使不間斷；此是功夫，成就者少。若能成就此心念心聽功夫、清晰分明而不間斷者，即須進一步探討：為何要心念心聽？若細細觀察思惟，便知心念心聽之目的，其實是在集中精神排遣妄想，當時憶佛之念若有似無，並不分明。有時乃至全無憶佛之念，而處於定境。既已觀察分明，便知轉折。此時應改心念心聽為心念心憶，配合心中連續不斷的佛號而保持憶想佛菩薩之淨念於不斷。當我們修學念佛法門到此一地步時，應已在念佛過程中，或多或少得到佛菩薩的冥感或顯相的感應，信心極強，不易退失。

四、無相念佛：此類人之所以能修學至無相念佛之層次，應已於過去生中恭敬供養　世尊、供養三寶，廣種福田、深植善根，並曾兼修禪定，淨定雙修而不偏廢。常親近善知識，卻絕不人云亦云。肯深入探索思惟念佛法門，而不斷地提昇自己的念佛層次。因此今生雖仍主修念佛法門，仍不忘攝取修定之知見；因淨土法門及修定法門之基本知見已具備故，於精進不斷的修學過程中，細法漸出，自然而然到達無相念佛之層次。心中憶佛之時，佛號、佛形了然不生。以具備深厚善根福慧之故，深知此種法門是真實念佛，毫無猶疑，一心決定，深入修持；自信必能於捨報之時以較高品位往生極樂淨土。此法即是《楞嚴經》中，〈大勢至菩薩念佛圓通章〉所說：「憶佛念佛，都攝六根，淨念相繼。」若能輔以無相憶念拜佛之方法，則可很容易地將無相念佛法門運用於日常生活中，而成就動靜之中皆能無相念佛之功夫。

　　一旦修成此種念佛法門，並能在日常生活中時時保持此種功夫者，我說此人對於佛法僧三寶，已經信心具足；於自己也一樣信心具足。此生必定不離三寶，出三界之家的心念油然而生。若有自修或共修時，持名憶佛極為精進，持念至無佛號可唸之際，爾時佛號不起，而能一心繫緣於所念之佛，心不散亂、憶念相續不斷者，則能體會此種境界。

　　如果此人能更精進，於此法門深入憶念、思惟、修習，清楚分明地了知：佛之形像非佛，佛之名號非佛，佛號之音聲非佛，乃至感應時佛所示現之佛形像非佛。佛者唯是一心，佛乃覺者。二千五百年前示現於印度之　釋迦牟尼佛，乃由法身所示現，是應化佛。佛之本際不生不滅，真實之佛不即空有而不離空有，唯是真心而已。是故吾人所念，既是此一心，心無名相，心無聲相，心無形相；我所念之佛，唯是此心，何須經由聲相、名相、形像來念佛呢？便於深心確定：念佛時應當捨離聲相、名相、形像而念佛。若念佛人能一心思惟、深入此知見者，便能捨離聲相、名相、形像而開始無相念佛，若能將此無相念佛之淨念由坐中移轉至日常生活中繼續練習者，則無相念佛之功夫可於一至三天之中初步成功。若極精進之人，繼續修習深入體會，一、二週乃至一、二月可以修至不憶而自憶之境地，憶佛之念猶如泉湧，源源不絕。無需刻意提撕此念，時時刻刻自然存在。

　　此憶佛之念雖然無相，然非憶十方佛，而是專憶特定之一尊佛。雖然無相，但是心中卻清楚分明地了知所憶之佛是哪一尊。此憶佛之念，以無相故，較難體會。若已有持名憶佛之功夫，則較容易體會。末學另以無相憶念拜佛之法以為佐助，幫助念佛人迅速深入此一境界。讀者欲知其詳，可函佛教正覺同修會索取《無相念佛》一書，以便深入探討。

欲修習無相念佛法門者，必須減少或消除攀緣心、覺觀心、疑心、慢心。若有攀緣心，則不能捨離名相、聲相、形像；即使能捨離，也不能保持淨念之相繼不斷。若不捨離覺觀之心，則會疑神疑鬼，或希求佛菩薩之感應，難以安住無相念佛（憶佛）之境界中，欲求淨念相繼，便不容易。

疑心不除，則懷疑此境界，認為無所根據；或疑此法非是佛法。此疑不除，則需等候十年、二十年，乃至五十年、一百年後，此法之弘傳已進入爛熟時期，彼方肯學。彼時或者垂垂老矣，或者已至來生，未必能遇此勝法，殊堪惋惜。卻不知古今大德闡述此法者不少；而末法時期流通佛書者，常以為此境界難以修成，而予以忽略，未能廣為弘揚；或有極少數人為方便故，將大德所述之「憶念」之旨，釋為持名，致念佛人多有所疑，裹足不前。

復有一種人難修此法，所謂「慢心」。此輩人或以禪為貴，花費一、二十年光陰，雖摸不到「話頭」，卻仍鍥而不捨，令人既敬佩又憐憫；或以皓首窮經為貴，成為佛學大家；時光荏苒，轉眼垂老。

此二種人往往懶於念佛，不樂與念佛人為伴。需知佛教以蓮花為象徵，非無因緣；蓮花象徵佛法之清淨尊貴，但蓮花卻於卑溼淤泥之中生長。學佛人若能去除慢心，則心謙卑、容易受法，修學念佛法門，易得成就。

末學自一九八九年五月起，以無相念佛法門助人學佛以來，深覺慢心之為害學佛人至深且鉅。若無慢心則修學迅速，得法容易。若有慢心，則往往流於權威崇拜，而不信任沒有名氣之善知識。即使真正善知識現前，亦不肯學，失之交臂。是故，欲深入念佛法門，必除慢心。

從事持達理持　即凡心是佛心

又此無相念佛法門雖名無相，仍非實相。以此念佛法捨離名相、聲相、形相故，相對於世俗之有相而施設此一無相念佛之名。

實相雖然無相，但無相不一定是實相；此中差別在於相對於有相而存在之無相，尚能以世俗之認識而了知；譬如無相念佛之無相、靈知心之無相、無色界眾生之無相、虛空之無相等。而實相則非世俗認識所能了知，譬如真如、佛性、菩提、涅槃。

大乘佛教所謂實相，非僅無相一端而已。乃是空有不二，是即相離相，無相無不相；不即空有二邊，而亦不離空有二邊，所謂中道。明心而不見性者，猶不能見此真實，何況凡夫之意識思惟，孰能至此？無相念佛雖然無相，仍非實相，而此境界，自古至今，真實有之。乃援引《大寶積經》卷四所載：「言無相者，所謂無身及身施設，無名無句亦無示現。」故施設此無相念佛之名，以便弘揚念佛法門，利益末法時代之念佛人與修禪人。

此無相念佛法門雖已無相，猶是因地念佛。設使無相念佛法門已經修成，憶佛之念猶如泉湧。

法喜之覺受則因時日之俱增而漸漸習慣、淡薄、消失。若能繼續無相念佛法門，必於某一時節突然一念迴光返照：「念佛者是誰？」或遇善知識冷冷一句：「念佛者是誰？」當下直得不辨東西南北，一頭栽進漆桶裡。從此每日孜孜矻矻體究此一疑情，猶如一團美味滾燙元宵，卡在嘴裡；吞又吞不下，捨也捨不下。此時憑藉無相念佛之深厚功夫，不必依賴語言文字，即能深入體究。有朝一日，突然悟得：「色身覺受、妄心妄識都不是我，那一念都無之真心，真實是我。」直下承當，毫無猶豫。從此識得一切生命之本源，見到那肉眼不能見得之真心，從此不以靈知為真。

如今突然打失鼻孔，有人因此哈哈大笑，有人因此喜極而泣，有人則不動聲色、安住真心之中。從此頓覺輕安無比，身心明淨。身（我）見頓時斷除。身（我）見斷故疑見隨斷，疑見斷故禁取見亦斷除。此三縛結斷故，其無相念佛即是果地念佛。雖是果地念佛，亦不過預流而已。既名預入聖流，即非真實聖者，猶執空性一邊以為真實。此即明心而未見性，尚未進入實相，即當求見佛性，進入實相念佛層次。

五、實相念佛：佛子修習念佛法門而能成就無相念佛者，殊不多見。今此無相念佛人復能究明真心，因體究念佛而得明心（開悟），斷三縛結，倍復可貴。而善知識給予印可後，多囑附弟子念佛保任而已。師徒之間，從此相安無事，浪擲光陰，徒耗米糧，殊可浩嘆。不知猶未親見佛性，仍須努力體究念佛。此一果地念佛之佛子若能知此，當即排遣萬緣，尋訪善知識。若有因緣得遇真善知識，此善知識當時聞其見地，考其過程，觀其根器之後，或者一掌打來，或者丟來一枚蘋果，或將拳指在念佛人眼前晃。念佛人若仍不見，便垂示一二句法語，令念佛人體究。

此念佛人若能精進奮發，努力參究，待得因緣時節到來，或者暖燙、或者寒涼、或者撞跌、或聞狗叫、或見花紅柳綠、或是歡喜悲痛，突然之間一念相應，識得佛性，再破無明。此時恍然發覺佛性無處不在，一時忍俊不住，摸摸頭頂，便笑自己以前真是愚癡，佛性本來就在眼前，以前竟然不覺。便到處看、隨處摸：無處不是佛性嘛！

若是打坐靜中體究，一念相應之後，隨即住於一切音聲中，細細體會佛性之無處不在。下座之後，亦到處體會其存在。到此時便知何謂禪淨雙修、禪淨互通了。佛子此時之境界，是遠離妄想雜念，一心住於覺照之中，遠離語言、文字、思惟法則、世間施設，無法形容，只一個「覺」字了得。此即理一心之境界，親見諸佛本源，即是見法身佛。從此開始，一連七天，乃至十個

七天，覺明時時現前，遠離昏沉散亂。平時不起
妄想，無一念可當情，而在色聲香味觸法之中，
覺照佛性之真空及其真實存在、能生萬有。夜晚
則不昏沉，躺在床舖、一念清明，乃至東方之既
白。或者清晨三、四點鐘便已醒來，了無睡意。
即起盥洗，燃香禮佛已畢，又自道：「我實從本
以來不曾拜佛。」從此以後，便見身心世界皆
是虛幻，真實感頓失。閱讀甚深第一義諦經典，
倍覺親切，猶如述說自心境界，若為他人敘述自
己所見境界，人皆以為此念佛人在解說甚深第一
義經典，便向此念佛人道：「別只在經論之名相
理論上追求，應該下功夫去實修。」真是啼笑皆
非。此外尚有許多功德受用，唯證乃知，不擬詳
述。

不假方便　自得心開

　　以上所述，係一般念佛人體究念佛（理持）之過程。然亦有根器猛利者，於明心之同時一念相應，得見佛性；不待善知識誘導，自得見佛法身；此即〈大勢至菩薩念佛圓通章〉所說：「若眾生心，憶佛念佛，『現前』當來，必定見佛」。

　　若是來生修到這個理一心的境界，便是「當來」必定見佛。這個見佛是見自性佛，見諸佛法身，見一切眾生之法身，而不是感應所見之化身佛。此時便恍然道：「原來諸佛法身竟是如此，一切眾生之本來面目亦復如此。」若此念佛人亦曾參禪，此時便道：「原來此是土城和尚立地處，好與三十拄杖。」

　　此一實相念佛之修持，從起疑到見性之全部體究過程，便是「不假方便，自得心開」。何以不假方便？實因憶佛念佛無相之故，與實相無相極為相應。無需學禪，自然會禪；無需學參話頭，自然會參話頭；無需揣摩擠破腦袋，自然能進入疑團；無需善知識，亦能自得心開。心開之過程有短至一天，有長達十餘年，乃至當來之世不等，故曰：「現前當來，必定見佛。」是謂「悟有遲疾，必定心開」也。

　　因為心開而見佛性之故，此後不論持名念佛、觀想念佛、無相念佛，皆是實相念佛。何以故？實相離一切相而即一切相故，實相非空非有、亦空亦有故。此時方可說「一句佛號概括事理」，因為念佛之事相與真理皆已通達，並能隨緣助人修學念佛法門。此時念佛，別是一番境界，不同於「心開」前之無相念佛。此時念佛，乃是以心念心；以我真心，念佛真心；能念所念，皆唯一心（編案：能念之心雖妄，然由真心而生，亦真心體性之一，故悟者之能念所念不二）。所差異者，在於佛之定慧圓滿，我未圓滿；佛之福慧具足，我未具足而已。展望前途，雖然永遠不再淪入三惡道，但是成佛之路猶甚遙遠，若憶佛時，便生慚愧；若憶念未到此境界之佛子，便覺悲憫，大悲之心油然而生，願助眾人循序而到。

　　到此地步者，欲求捨報之時，上品上生往生極樂淨土，必蒙　彌陀世尊攝受。捨報之前，安慰預告；捨報時至，坐金剛臺，往生極樂；應時得見彌陀世尊，頓悟無生法忍。能於須臾之間，親到十方世界禮拜供養無量數佛；在諸佛前次第受記，即還極樂淨土，得無量百千陀羅尼大總持門。

　　念佛人修學至此，已得極大功德受用和解脫，譬如：當眾受辱，心中亦能真實無瞋，不予理會。

雖然如此，佛子猶不可心滿；於幫助佛子們念佛之餘，應續修學廣義之念佛法門。主要方向是修學種智及根本四禪；佛子已入實相故，煩惱幾已消除殆盡，修學四禪可以快過他人十百千倍。四禪若得，應續修學觀禪、鍊禪、熏禪、修禪。此皆是定，因定而生無量百千三昧，邁向佛道，利益無量眾生。莫以實相念佛境界為足，停滯不前。

釋疑：或有人言：「此文談念佛，不應說禪。」此則應說念佛層次提升時之轉折。譬如持名念佛之人，多停留於心唸心聽之階段，不知轉為心唸心憶。已能心唸心憶後，應轉為無相憶佛，捨離一切相。乃竟有人因憶佛時，佛號不起而生煩惱，此即不知轉折也。待無相念佛（憶佛）之念如泉湧現而不斷時，便應體究念佛，即是由事持轉為理持，此亦是轉折。吾人嘗見知見不足者或排斥修禪者，於此煩惱退縮，停於無相念佛之境界，錯失「見佛」因緣，不入實相念佛境界；上品上生之果報，失之交臂，極為可惜。此皆知見不足，不知轉折之過也。

佛法雖然廣有八萬四千解脫法門，但每一法門之修持，到最後都必與第一義諦（實相）相應。不論是天台之止觀，禪宗之參禪，淨土之念佛……等；任何一種法門，若有因緣修持到第一義現前，其最後階段修持過程之本質莫非是禪。

而每一法門之修持，自初始、至終了，皆必有其轉折。那便是由散亂心到統一心，定力現前。因定力現前並起心探究，而得見真心之空性，此即明心（開悟）；由見無所見、明了真心，繼續體究而見佛性，實相現前；智慧於此顯現，能使他人受益。

　　此種轉折過程、因各種修持方式之不同而呈現不同之相貌，但其原理則一。換言之；禪存在於每一種解脫法門之最後階段，非獨禪宗有之。到達此階段之前的漫長修持，其目的皆在增強定力和知見。定力與知見俱足，便知轉折。一旦因緣成熟，禪就出現了。

　　簡單的說，便是「攝心為戒，因戒生定，由定發慧」而得解脫。其轉折之原理便是從有相到無相，因權巧而入實相。既入實相，則無相無不相；是故天台宗說「理事不二」，禪宗說「山色無非清淨身，溪聲即是廣長舌」，淨土宗說「一句佛號概括事理」等等。此種轉折原理和原則，不論任何宗派，一體通用。譬如　世尊於經中所說位於此娑婆世界東方之不眴世界，其世界中無有文字及言說之施設，而於彼世界之佛仍然能夠以法化導諸菩薩。無有文字及言說之施設，猶如修學無相念佛者，於開始時不將念佛之念繫於文字相以及持名唸佛之言說聲相，慢慢修練而轉進，乃至轉入參話頭，成就體究念佛，最後得以親證法界實相，即是藉著無相念佛為方便化導菩薩悟道明心。茲舉示《大乘理趣六波羅蜜多經》卷二中世尊之開示做為佐證：

> 爾時薄伽梵復告具壽阿難陀言：「彼不眴世界無諸苦難，及三惡趣亦不聞名……國土嚴淨，唯佛法王化諸菩薩，無有文字亦無言說。彼諸菩薩受化之時，來詣佛所恭敬合掌，目不蹔眴瞻仰如來，念佛三昧自然成就，故彼世界名為不眴。念佛三昧云何是耶？所謂非色相生，亦非受想行識生，非前後邊際智慧生，亦非現在見聞所生。」佛告阿難「其念佛三摩地不可思議，於諸法無所行而觀諸法如實相，無說無示、無相無名，此即名為念佛三昧。」

如所舉經文中 世尊所說之不眴世界，無有文字亦無有言說，彼世界諸菩薩親近佛、接受佛之化導時，只要恭敬合掌，目不轉睛的瞻仰 如來，念佛三昧便自然成就了，當時就能悟得離於語言文字之自性彌陀，亦即由無相之方便直接進入了實相。而此處既未有唸佛持名之施設，為何經中卻說已經成就了念佛三昧？可見體究念佛之真實義，在於求證實相、參究實相之過程，此即是體究念佛；而念佛之本質即是要見真實佛—親證法界實相—才是見佛之真實義。何以故？因為 世尊說念佛三昧不是從色、受、想、行、識之法相所生，也不是從諸緣所安立的十二因緣法獲得之智慧所生，也不是現前所見所聞之見聞覺知法所生。念佛三昧是意識所不可思不可議的，當現前與一向不行見聞覺知、離見聞覺知的自性彌陀一念相應，以般若智慧觀察到自性彌陀就是五蘊諸法出生的根源時，現見自性彌陀本來無生，而自性彌陀所含藏的蘊處界法種及具足種種功德法性，亦同樣本來無生，能隨順因緣而出生五蘊諸法，此即是諸法之如實法相，故說自性彌陀是諸法之實相，能現觀諸法如實法相之智慧就是念佛三昧。知此道理，便能於修持各種解脫法門時，知所抉擇，迅速入道。

誠懇的叮嚀：修學念佛法門之初期，但能參加定期共修，參閱善知識著作，配合平時持名念佛之功夫，便得受用。若欲精進修持到無相念佛階段，其修行過程中，有少數人可能發生感應現象，譬如見光，聞香，見佛示現金身……等；固然可喜，但勿執著。極少數人（萬不及一）若有定中見佛說法，指導修行者，務須依三法印及四依法印證；若不相應，慎勿遵從，便都無事。部份人則於無相念佛修持純熟後，發生輕安、清涼、喜悅、悲憫、消除慢心、入定……等現象，此皆是定心之顯現，無需驚惶掛礙，繼續深入修習即可。

　　又：近年來，曾遇數位學佛人，或因參禪、或因體究念佛而至無語言文字妄想之境界時，便將無相念佛之心勇敢承擔，便以「此心為我」呈善知識，善知識便以此印證為開悟，渾然不知此心仍是妄心。若「離語言文字妄想便是真心」，則一切無語言妄想傍生之心皆離語言文字妄想，一切修定有成者亦能離語言文字妄想，彼等靈覺心亦應是真心；若謂彼為真心，則彼等對於明心所具之解脫功德受用，為何遲不現前？此微細處，務須真善知識始得明辨，並善導行者知見、以趣正道。莫以靈知心之無念為悟，莫以定境見花（心花）為悟，否則，明心之空尚不可得，遑論進入實相之空有不二境界。

　　是故行者若欲體究念佛時，最好有真善知識指導。所謂真善知識，是指此人已入實相念佛境界，親見佛性而不退失，於第一義諦真實了知；並有方便善巧，能教導念佛人從有相入無相，藉權巧入實相。此善知識未必有名氣，卻能引導念佛人之修行於前，能勘驗念佛人之境界於後；避免體究念佛者誤將妄心作為真心，免將妄覺誤作真覺。能使念佛人順次進入實相念佛境界，並消除念佛人對於聖境之執著。所幸此種善知識，在台灣已日漸增加，尋覓不難。要緊的是我們念佛同修能否建立信心、消滅慢心、發菩提心、行菩薩行。否則，即使善知識現前，亦恐當面錯過。

　　以上所述是由持名念佛而入之事持及理持五種層次。無相念佛雖然不易修成，但是若有方便善巧，按部就班，努力練習，其實不難。實相念佛雖非大多數人可以想望，然非絕無可能。若能修成無相念佛三昧，時時精勤護念，袪除慢心，善發菩薩大心，每日跪求　　釋迦世尊指示善知識之因緣及所在，必有一日得見有緣，亦有可能於三言兩語之下決了。若不得善知識，是因緣尚不具足，無需氣餒，只要細細體究，縱使現前不見，至少得保人身，當來必定見佛。

　　若真是菩薩種性者，往往能於修成無相念佛三昧之後二、三年內自修自悟，親見實相，能於經論之中多方印證。若不發菩薩大心，不去除慢心懦心、而求實相念佛境界者，無有是處。願誠摯地在此與一切佛子共勉：「普願佛子憶佛念佛，現前當來皆得見佛，心量廣大饒益有情。」

　　　　　　　　　　菩薩戒子　蕭平實　敬筆

CHARTS: THE CULTIVATION STAGES WITHIN THE TWO MAIN PATHS OF BUDDHA BODHI (ENGLISH & CHINESE)

The Cultivation Stages of the Two Paths within the Buddha Bodhi

The joint cultivation of these two paths is the one and only way to attain Buddhahood

	The Great Bodhi: Path to Buddhahood		The Bodhi of the Two Lesser Vehicles: Path to Liberation
Path of Accumulation	Ten Faiths: Bodhisattvas accumulate faith in the Buddha Dharma. This will take one to ten thousand eons to accomplish.	Extensively practicing the six *pāramitās* before achieving awakening to the True Mind.	
	First Abiding: Bodhisattvas accumulate virtues of charitable giving, primarily material goods.		Practitioners eliminate the three fetters to attain the first fruition of liberation.
	Second Abiding: Bodhisattvas accumulate virtues of precept observance.		
	Third Abiding: Bodhisattvas accumulate virtues of forbearance.		
	Fourth Abiding: Bodhisattvas accumulate virtues of diligence.		
	Fifth Abiding: Bodhisattvas accumulate virtues of meditative absorption.		
Distant Pāramitās ▲	Sixth Abiding: Bodhisattvas accumulate virtues of *prajñā* by studying and familiarizing themselves with the Middle Way of *prajñā* and eliminating the view of self during the Path of Preparation.		
	Seventh Abiding: Bodhisattvas awaken to the True Mind and gain direct comprehension of *prajñā*, thereupon realize directly the nirvana with primordial, intrinsic and pure nature.	Extensively practicing the six *pāramitās* after achieving awakening to the True Mind.	Practitioners attain the second fruition of liberation by reducing greed, aversion, and delusion.
First Faith to Tenth Dedication	Eighth Abiding: Starting from this stage, bodhisattvas gain direct comprehension of the Middle Way of *prajñā* in all phenomena, and gradually eliminate their dispositional hindrances.		
	Tenth Abiding: Bodhisattvas see the Buddha-nature with the physical eye and attain direct comprehension of the illusoriness of the world.		
Path of Vision	First Practice to Tenth Practice: While extensively cultivating the six *pāramitās*, bodhisattvas rely on their insights into the Middle Way of *prajñā* to directly comprehend the aggregates, sense-fields, and elements are illusory like mirages. Upon completing the Tenth Practice, they will have fully accomplished the direct comprehension of these phenomena being like mirages.		Practitioners attain the third fruition of liberation by eliminating the five lower fetters.
	First Dedication to Tenth Dedication: Bodhisattvas study and familiarize themselves with the knowledge-of-all-aspects and eliminate dispositional hindrances, except the last bit of affliction eradicated through cultivation. Upon completing the Tenth Dedication, they will have attained direct comprehension of the bodhisattva path being like a dream.		

Near Pāramitās ▲ **First Ground to Seventh Ground**	**Path of Vision**	First Ground: Upon completing the Tenth Dedication, bodhisattvas will have realized a portion of the knowledge-of-the-aspects-of-paths, consisting of personal and direct realization of each of the eight consciousnesses, which enables them to perceive the five aspects of dharmas, the three natures, the seven facets of the ultimate truth, the seven intrinsic natures [of the *tathāgatagarbha*], and the two types of selflessness. They enter the Stage of Proficiency (First Ground) after bravely making the ten inexhaustible vows. Also, they can attain liberation from samsara through wisdom at this point, they purposely retain the last bit of affictive hindrances to nourish future rebirths out of their great vows. The principal cultivation of the First Ground consists of the *pāramitā* of Dharma teaching as well as the Hundred Dharmas. The cultivation of the First Ground is completed when bodhisattvas attain direct comprehension of the six sense-objects being like images in a mirror.	Before entering the First Ground, bodhisattvas undertake the four levels of intensified efforts to eradicate the manifestation of all afflictive hindrances and attain the fourth fruition of liberation. However, the last bit of affictive hindrances is purposely retained to nourish future rebirths. Bodhisattvas have put an end to delimited existence (*pariccheda-jarāmaraṇa*) and proceed to eliminate the habitual seeds of afflictive hindrances, as well as the higher afflictions of beginningless ignorance.
	Path of Cultivation	Second Ground: Bodhisattvas enter the Second Ground when they have completed their cultivation of the First Ground and realized an additional portion of the knowledge-of-the-aspects-of-paths. Cultivation of this stage focuses on the *pāramitā* of precept observance and the knowledge-of-all-aspects. Upon completing the Second Ground, bodhisattvas will have attained direct comprehension of the first seven consciousnesses being like light and shadows. Thereupon, they will be able to adhere to precepts in a way that is both pure and natural.	
		Third Ground: Bodhisattvas advance to the Third Ground after having realized an additional portion of the knowledge-of-the-aspects-of-paths upon completing the Second Ground. The principal cultivation of the Third Ground includes the *pāramitā* of forbearance, the four concentrations and the four formless absorptions, the four boundless minds, as well as the five supernatural powers. While bodhisattvas on the Third Ground can realize the fruition of twofold liberation, they deliberately choose not to; instead, they purposely retain the last bit of affictive hindrances to nourish future rebirths. Upon completing the Third Ground, bodhisattvas will have attained direct comprehension of all voices of Dharma teaching being like echoes in a valley and achieved the mind-made body attained through the taintless and wondrous *samādhi*.	
		Fourth Ground: Bodhisattvas advance to the Fourth Ground after having realized an additional portion of the knowledge-of-the-aspects-of-paths on the Third Ground. The principal cultivation of this stage is the *pāramitā* of diligence, for which bodhisattvas extensively and tirelessly teach and guide sentient beings who have karmic connections with them in this and other worlds. They will also continue their cultivation of the knowledge-of-all-aspects. Upon completing the Fourth Ground, bodhisattvas will have attained direct comprehension of their own mind-made bodies generated during *samādhi* being like the moon reflected in water.	
		Fifth Ground: Bodhisattvas advance to the Fifth Ground after having realized an additional portion of the knowledge-of-the-aspects-of-paths on the Fourth Ground. The *pāramitā* of meditative absorption and the knowledge-of-all-aspects constitute the principal cultivation of the Fifth Ground. Bodhisattvas will also eliminate the desire for nirvana possessed by adherents of the lesser vehicles. Upon completing the Fifth Ground, they will have attained direct comprehension of all bodhisattvas' mind-made bodies and emanation bodies being like the effects of conjuring.	

Near Pāramitās ▲	Sixth Ground: Bodhisattvas advance to the Sixth Ground after having realized an additional portion of the knowledge-of-the-aspects-of-paths on the Fifth Ground. The principal cultivation of the Sixth Ground is the *pāramitā* of *prajñā*: relying on the knowledge-of-the-aspects-of-paths they have acquired, bodhisattvas directly comprehend that each of the twelve factors of dependent arising as well as the mind-made and emanation bodies are all transformations of one's mind of True Suchness, and therefore are "seemingly but not truly existent." Having accomplished the contemplation of the subtle characteristics of these dharmas, they acquire the ability to spontaneously realize the meditative absorption of cessation without any added effort. Thereupon, they become Mahāyāna adepts (*aśaikṣa*) of twofold liberation.	Upon completing the Seventh Ground, bodhisattvas will have eliminated the last bit of "affliction" that has been purposely retained. They will also have thoroughly eliminated all tainted habitual seeds of afflictive hindrances associated with the aggregates of form, sensation, and perception.
First Ground to Seventh Ground	Seventh Ground: After attaining direct comprehension of the transformations of one's own mind of True Suchness being "seemingly but not truly existent" on the Sixth Ground, bodhisattvas attain an additional portion of the knowledge-of-the-aspects-of-paths and advance to the Seventh Ground. The cultivation of the Seventh Ground focuses on continued learning of the knowledge-of-all-aspects and the *pāramitā* of skillful means. Additionally, bodhisattvas contemplate again all the subtle characteristics of each of the twelve factors of dependent arising from the perspectives of transmigration and the extinction of transmigration, whereby they achieve mastery of skillful means and the ability to enter the meditative absorption of cessation in a single thought. Upon completing the Seventh Ground, bodhisattvas will have attained direct comprehension of the nirvana they have realized being as illusory as a *gandharva's* city.	
Path of Cultivation	Eighth Ground: Having attained the contemplation of the extremely subtle characteristics on the Seventh Ground, bodhisattvas realize an additional portion of the knowledge-of-the-aspects-of-paths and advance to the Eighth Ground. The principal cultivation of the Eighth Ground concentrates on the continued learning of the knowledge-of-all-aspects and the *pāramitā* of vows. Upon completing the Eighth Ground, bodhisattvas will be able to spontaneously bring forth the exclusively signless contemplation at all times and hence can manipulate physical objects or mental images at will. Also, they will have realized the mind-made body attained through correct realization of dharma characteristics.	
Great Pāramitās ▲	Ninth Ground: Bodhisattvas advance to the Ninth Ground after having realized an additional portion of the knowledge-of-the-aspects-of-paths on the Eighth Ground. The principal cultivation of the Ninth Ground consists of the *pāramitā* of strength as well as continued learning of the knowledge-of-all-aspects. Upon completing the Ninth Ground, bodhisattvas will have mastered the four unhindered knowledges and realized the mind-made body attained without added effort and in accordance with the classes of beings to be delivered.	Bodhisattvas gradually and spontaneously eliminate the taintless habitual seeds of afflictive hindrances associated with the aggregates of formation and consciousness, as well as the higher afflictions of cognitive hindrances.
Eighth Ground to Virtual Enlightenment	Tenth Ground: Bodhisattvas advance to the Tenth Ground after having realized an additional portion of the knowledge-of-the-aspects-of-paths on the Ninth Ground. The principal cultivation of the Tenth Ground is the knowledge-of-all-aspects, namely, the *pāramitā* of omniscience. Upon completing the Tenth Ground, bodhisattvas will be able to generate the cloud of great Dharma wisdom and manifest the various meritorious qualities contained therein. They will also become a "designated bodhisattva."	

Great Pāramitās	Path of Cultivation	Virtual Enlightenment: After having realized the portion of the knowledge-of-the-aspects-of-paths cultivated on the Tenth Ground, bodhisattvas advance to the stage of Virtual Enlightenment. At this stage, they cultivate the knowledge-of-all-aspects and perfectly realize the acquiescence to the non-arising of dharmas (*anutpattikadharmakṣānti*) pertaining to this stage. They will also perfect the thirty-two majestic physical features and innumerable associated good marks unique to Buddha by cultivating and accumulating enormous amount of virtues over a hundred eons.	Bodhisattvas gradually and spontaneously eliminate the taintless habitual seeds of afflictive hindrances associated with the aggregates of formation and consciousness, as well as the higher afflictions of cognitive hindrances.	
Perfect Pāramitās	Path of Ultimate Realization	Sublime Enlightenment: Bodhisattvas have thoroughly eliminated all habitual seeds of afflictive hindrances and all latent cognitive hindrances, as well as permanently eradicated the ignorance that leads to transformational existence. They will manifest birth in the human world, realize the great nirvana, and perfect the four kinds of wisdom of Buddha. After displaying physical death in the human world, their reward-bodies will permanently reside in the highest heaven of the form-realm to continue to teach and guide bodhisattvas on or above the First Ground coming from all worlds. Having accomplished the ultimate fruition of Buddhahood, they will generate numerous emanation bodies to perpetually teach and guide sentient beings.	Bodhisattvas bring transformational existence (*parinamikijarāmaraṇa*) to a complete end and attain the great nirvana.	

Perfect Ultimate Fruition of Buddhahood
Respectfully composed by Buddhist disciple Xiao Pingshi (Feb. 2012)

佛菩提二主要道次第概要表

二道並修，以外無別佛法

		佛菩提道——大菩提道		解脫道：二乘菩提
遠波羅蜜多：初信至十迴向	資糧位	十信位修集信心——一劫乃至一萬劫		
		初住位修集布施功德（以財施為主）。	外門廣修六度萬行	斷三縛結，成初果解脫
		二住位修集持戒功德。		
		三住位修集忍辱功德。		
		四住位修集精進功德。		
		五住位修集禪定功德。		
		六住位修集般若功德（熏習般若中觀及斷我見，加行位也。）		
	見道位	七住位明心般若正觀現前，親證本來自性清淨涅槃。		
		八住位起於一切法現觀般若中道。漸除性障性。		
		十住位眼見佛性，世界如幻觀成就。	內門廣修六度萬行	薄貪瞋癡，成二果解脫
		一至十行位，於廣行六度萬行中，依般若中道慧，現觀陰處界猶如陽焰，至第十行滿心位，陽焰觀成就。		
		一至十迴向位熏習一切種智；消除性障，唯留最後一分思惑不斷。第十迴向位滿心成就菩薩道如夢觀。		斷五下分結，成三果解脫

	內容	斷惑
		入地前的四加行令煩惱障現行悉斷，留惑潤生。分段生死已斷，煩惱障習氣種子開始無明上煩惱。兼斷。
	→	
見道位	初地：第十週向位滿心時，成就道種智一分（八識心王一一親證後，領受五法、三自性、七種第一義、七種性自性，二種無我法）復由勇發十無盡願，成通達位菩薩，此地主修法施波羅蜜多及百法明門。證「猶如鏡像」現觀，故滿初地心。	七地滿心斷除故意保留之最後一分思惑時，受、想三陰所攝色、煩惱障所有有漏習氣種子同時斷盡。
修道位	二地：初地功德滿足以後，再成就道種智一分而入二地；主修戒波羅蜜多及一切種智。滿心位成就「猶如光影」現觀。戒行自然清淨。	
	三地：二地滿心再證道種智一分，故入三地。此地主修忍波羅蜜多及四禪八定、四無量心、五神通。能成就俱解脫果而不取證，留惑潤生。滿心位成就「猶如谷響」現觀及無漏妙定意生身。	
	四地：由三地再證道種智一分故入四地。主修精進波羅蜜多，於此土及他方世界廣度有緣，無有疲倦。進修一切種智，滿心位成就「如水中月」現觀。	
	五地：由四地再證道種智一分故入五地。主修禪定波羅蜜多及一切種智，斷除下乘涅槃貪。滿心位成就「變化所成」現觀。	
	六地：由五地再證道種智一分故入六地。此地主修般若波羅蜜多及一切種智十二因緣——一一有支皆自心真如變化所現，「非有似有」，成就細相觀，不由加行而自然證得滅盡定。滿心位證得「似有非有」現觀。	
近波羅蜜多：初地至七地	七地：由六地「非有似有」現觀，再證道種智一分故入七地。此地主修一切種智及方便波羅蜜多，由重觀十二有支一一支中之流轉門及還滅門一切細相，成就方便善巧，念念隨入滅盡定。滿心位證得「如犍闥婆城」現觀。	

	八地至等覺 大波羅蜜多： 修道位				圓滿波羅蜜多 究竟位	
	八地：由七地極細相觀成就故再證道種智一分而入八地。此地主修一切種智及頗波羅蜜多。至滿心位純無相觀任運相起，故於相土自在，滿心位復證「如實覺知諸法相意生身」故。	九地：由八地再證道種智一分故入九地。主修力波羅蜜多及一切種智，成就四無礙，滿心位證得「種類俱生無行作意生身」。	十地：由九地再證道種智一分故入此地。此地主修一切種智——智波羅蜜多。滿心位起大法智雲，及現起大法智雲所含藏種種功德，成受職菩薩。	等覺：由十地道種智成就故入此地。此地應修一切種智，圓滿等覺地無生法忍：於百劫中集極廣大福德，以之圓滿三十二大人相及無量隨形好。	妙覺：示現受生人間已斷盡煩惱障一切習氣種子，並斷盡所知障一切隨眠，永斷變易生死，成就大般涅槃。四智圓明，人間捨壽後，報身常住色究竟天利樂十方地上菩薩；以諸化身利樂有情，永無盡期，成就究竟佛道。	煩惱障所攝行、識二陰無漏習氣種子任運漸斷，所知障任運上煩惱任運漸斷。 斷盡變易生死，成就大般涅槃。

圓滿成就究竟佛果

佛子蕭平實 謹製 (2012年2月)

CULTIVATION CENTERS OF THE TRUE ENLIGHTENMENT PRACTITIONERS ASSOCIATION

Taipei True Enlightenment Lecture Hall
9F, No. 277, Sec. 3, Chengde Rd., Taipei 103, Taiwan, R.O.C.
Tel.: +886-2-2595-7295
(Ext. 10 & 11 for 9F; 15 & 16 for 10F; 18 & 19 for 5F; and 14 for the bookstore on 10F.)

Daxi True Enlightenment Patriarch Hall
No. 5-6, Kengdi, Ln. 650, Xinyi Rd., Daxi Township, Taoyuan County 335, Taiwan, R.O.C.
Tel.: +886-3-388-6110

Taoyuan True Enlightenment Lecture Hall
10F, No. 286 & 288, Jieshou Rd., Taoyuan 330, Taiwan, R.O.C.
Tel.: +886-3-374-9363

Hsinchu True Enlightenment Lecture Hall
2F-1, No. 55, Dongguang Rd., Hsinchu 300, Taiwan, R.O.C.
Tel.: +886-3-572-4297

Taichung True Enlightenment Lecture Hall
13F-4, No. 666, Sec. 2, Wuquan W. Rd., Nantun Dist., Taichung 408, Taiwan, R.O.C.
Tel.: +886-4-2381-6090

Jiayi True Enlightenment Lecture Hall
8F-1, No. 288, Youai Rd., Jiayi 600, Taiwan, R.O.C.
Tel.: +886-5-231-8228

Tainan True Enlightenment Lecture Hall
4F, No. 15, Sec. 4, Ximen Rd., Tainan 700, Taiwan, R.O.C.
Tel.: +886-6-282-0541

Kaohsiung True Enlightenment Lecture Hall
5F, No. 45, Zhongzheng 3rd Rd., Kaohsiung 800, Taiwan, R.O.C.
Tel.: +886-7-223-4248

Los Angeles True Enlightenment Lecture Hall
825 S. Lemon Ave, Diamond Bar, CA 91789, U.S.A.
Tel.: +1-909-595-5222
Cell: +1-626-454-0607

Hong Kong True Enlightenment Lecture Hall
Unit E1, 27th Floor, TG Place, 10 Shing Yip Street, Kwun Tong, Kowloon, Hong Kong
Tel: +852-2326-2231

Website of the True Enlightenment Practitioners Association:
http://www.enlighten.org.tw

Website of the True Wisdom Publishing Co.:
http://books.enlighten.org.tw

Readers may download free publications of the Association from the above website.